The New Tibetan-English Dictionary of Modern Tibetan